CLOCKWORK

EASY GIFT CLOCKS TO MAKE

CLOCKWORK

EASY GIFT CLOCKS TO MAKE

TIMOTHY BERTRAM

PIATKUS

© 1987 Timothy Bertram

First published in 1987 by
Judy Piatkus (Publishers) Limited,
5 Windmill Street, London W1P 1HS

British Library Cataloguing in Publication Data

Bertram, Timothy
   Clockwork: easy gift clocks to make
   4. Clock and watch making——
   ——Amateur's manuals
   I. Title
   681.1'13   TS545

   ISBN 0–86188–677–1

Designed and illustrated by Paul Saunders
Photography by Tim Imrie

Typeset by Phoenix Photosetting, Chatham, Kent
Printed and bound by The Bath Press, Avon

Contents

INTRODUCTION

Times Gone By

The measurement of time goes back into history and beyond. In Britain we were rather backward, and only started counting the hours 4000 years ago on our oldest surviving clock, Stonehenge. This was a particularly sophisticated model as it showed not only the time and date, but also the position of the sun and stars as well.

In Sumneer at the mouth of the river Tigris, and in Egypt the same sort of clocks were being built a couple of thousand years earlier. These great calendar clocks take years to set up and are a bit slow-moving for our modern tastes, but they are very easy to make if you have the space and time. Firstly, place a large stone or a good stout stake in the middle of your garden so that it casts a shadow. Then, over the next year, mark the tip of the shadow at midday on important dates like family birthdays and anniversaries. If you watch that shadow at midday all the following year, you will know when it is your birthday, because the shadow will fall exactly where you marked it the year before. Not very handy, but fun. The great Victorian engineer, Isembard Kingdom Brunel used this idea and built a long railway tunnel; at dawn on his birthday, the sun shines right through that tunnel. Most of us, however, must live with lesser timepieces for lesser events.

Eventually even the Egyptians felt they needed something more convenient than monolithic structures to break up the day, so they invented the water clock: a simple bowl with a hole, which was filled with water. As the water slowly leaked away, the remaining level indicated the time. Unfortunately, changes of temperature made the water escape at different speeds, which meant that some hours were longer than others. They then discovered that sand was more consistent than water, and so was born the hour glass, which continued in use right through the Middle Ages, and even into modern times as the common egg timer. All sorts of other ingenious devices were tried, such as King Alfred's candle: he put marks at regular spaces down the side of an ordinary candle. As it burned away, the level of the wax dropped to his marks, and in this way he divided up his working day. This was not particularly accurate, either. The rate at which wax melts depends upon the intensity of the flame and the length of the wick, among other factors. As the wick constantly changes, and as environmental conditions affect the flame, it is surprising that King Alfred was ever on time for anything.

Apart from King Alfred's candle, there was the sun dial in all its many forms, casting a shadow right across the history of time keeping. In this basic form, they are so simple that they were put on many, if not most, important buildings. Unfortunately, however beautiful and ornate they may be, they do not work when there is no sun or at night, which accounts for most of the time anywhere in the world.

Why did people go to all that trouble to measure time in the first place? What did it matter? There were, after all, no trains to catch, and work went on from first light until dark. The answer is religion. In early times the sun, as the source of all life, was an important symbol and any movement or change such as an eclipse was most significant. A priest who could foretell such events was both useful and powerful. In more sophisticated religions, keeping to timetables of prayer became essential, and great effort was put into means of telling the time accurately.

At the beginning of this millennium in Europe, the great cathedrals and abbeys kept a time keeper who watched his sundial and turned his hourglass. On each hour he hit a bell, so that the monks would know when to go to prayer. In the 13th century, however, a new type of weight-driven clock first appeared, which made time keepers redundant. One of the first was in use at Canterbury in 1292, followed by Salisbury and Wells in c. 1300, and then Norwich in 1323. At first these early movements drove mechanical men, known as Jacks, who hit a bell. Later on, dials were added and later still the mechanisms were improved, and then replaced altogether. Although in many old towns we can still see these old Jacks working, they are driven by more recent mechanisms.

The first great clocks, several of which can be seen in The Science Museum in London, were made of wrought iron and appear extremely crude to our modern eyes. Their speed was controlled by a simple escapement, which was subject to all sorts of variables, such as the wind and the weather. It is in this escapement that the long story of clock development lies. For 300 years clock – makers tried and tried to control the exact speed of the mechanism and then, in 1657, Christian Hugyens invented the pendulum, which was a great swing forward! By now, it was not only the Church that pushed for improvement, but also the clockmakers them-selves who simply wanted to beat their rivals, and the Navy who desperately needed a very

accurate clock for ships to calculate their position. In fact, the British government offered a prize of £10,000 in 1714, a lot of money in those days, for a clock that was accurate enough to be only one degree out after a voyage from England to the West Indies and back.

Because clocks were so inaccurate, they had to be reset regularly, but as there was no radio or television the only sure way of doing this was by the sun. Everyone used local solar time; lesser and private clocks were set from the striking of the central town or church clock. This meant, for example, that Bristol was ten minutes behind London, but as no one could be in both places at once, or know what the other place thought the time was, it did not matter. Within London, or rather Clerkenwell, which was the centre of the clock industry, clocks were set from Greenwich. Greenwich had been established by Charles II in 1675 to study astronomy and use it to improve navigation. It was therefore the best equipped place to observe the sun. To save each separate clockmaker from having to travel to Greenwich, a 19th century character called John Belville took his watch, *Mr Arnold*, three times a week to be set there, and on his return he sold the time to his customers. This service was later continued by his daughter Ruth.

With the beginning of the railways, it began to matter that different towns had different times. In fact, at one time, timetables were printed with dual times, which was all very confusing. The Great Western Railway was so keen that its trains should be on time that it had special clocks made, two for each guard: one that ran slowly for trains going west, and another that ran fast for trains going east! Matters became so complicated that eventually, in 1880, Parliament passed an act making Greenwich time standard for all the

British Isles. Still, how were people who didn't live in Greenwich supposed to know what the time was in Greenwich? In London this was solved in 1859 by the building of Big Ben at the cost of £4080. Even then, it was not exact for people living any distance away, as the sound took five seconds per mile to reach them. To overcome this, special maps were printed, with concentric rings showing one-second intervals radiating out from Big Ben.

For the rest of the country, the electric telegraph was used to link railway stations and post offices with Greenwich time. This went on until 1926 when at last everyone could get the exact time from the radio, and Ruth Belville stopped going to Greenwich.

But still we continue with more and more accurate ways of recording time. Now, for the first time, time is not only more accurate, but cheaper too. A petrol station watch costs less than £2 and keeps extremely good time. Or alternatively, for £4–£5 we can buy a movement which will drive any clock we care to make. . .

Making Time

The modern quartz movements specified throughout this book are extremely versatile and, within obvious limits, fairly tough. Although they are not exactly heatproof or waterproof, they could withstand the heat and damp of a bathroom or kitchen. They make it easy for people with the minimum of manual dexterity to create an enormous variety of clocks. Everyone has some material that they are able to work with, and which they like, and practically any material can be used as the basis for one of these clocks. How these movements work, and why they keep such good time, does not concern us here. All we need to know is that they work, they are cheap, they run for about eighteen months on one small battery, and they leave us to concentrate on far more interesting things like the case and the external design.

One of the most exciting aspects of this enterprise is its great potential for presents. At times we have all wondered what on earth we could give to some relation or friend, and here is the perfect answer. These clocks will make gifts that give us the pleasure of designing and making, knowing that the recipient will think of us whenever they look at the time. Particularly in the case of grandparents and older relatives, the fact that the gift was actually made by us adds an enormous bonus. Incidentally, it also makes them emotionally blind to any slight imperfections in the construction! Another advantage of making clocks to give as presents is that they can be personalised. Discreet initials in gold paint on a plate, with a birth date alongside will make a charming present for the parents of a newly born or newly christened child. Using the instructions given for the *Fabric Clock*, you could embroider a name and date, and then turn your tapestry into a clock. Birthdays, anniversaries, weddings – plates, cloth, perspex – the possibilities are endless.

When a great craftsman makes anything, he

will strive to produce it as well as he possibly can, and we are all impressed that something can be made so beautifully. But the craftsman will always see where he might have made it a little better, and the next time he will try to better it. The same applies to us: we must make our clocks as well as we can, but always try to produce a better one next time. It doesn't matter how clumsy you are at first; remember that the worst step we ever took in life was our first, but our parents were thrilled by it! No matter how impractical or unhandy you think you are, have a go.

I have tried to give you tips on how to set about using a variety of different materials and designs, but I hope that you will interpret this advice into your own schemes and ideas. Each clock in this book could generate a hundred more, all based on the same instructions, but totally different in effect. Colours and shapes and textures are things that each individual feels differently about. There is tradition and fashion and good taste, but most important of all are your own likes and dislikes. Use the simple principles behind each set of instructions in this book to unleash your personal clockmaking skills; if you like a particular colour, go ahead and paint your clock that colour!

If you have an old clock with a defunct engine or happen to pick one up at a junkshop, a quartz movement is the easiest way of restoring it to working order. Just rip out the engine, throw it away, and fit the new one. Once you have grasped the principle behind these 13 clocks, replacing an old movement is as easy as that. Obviously there are certain fundamental factors to bear in mind. You should buy hands that will fit inside the glass door that protects the dial, and you will normally need a short spindle movement, or else the door will not close. A chiming device is usually suitable, but remember that your clock will not tick audibly unless you have a second hand. However, this book is not about restoration. At the moment there is such a fashion for vintage clocks that the price has risen far too high for our amateur hands to tamper and experiment with these mini treasures. If you do decide to alter a clock, please consult a clockmaker before doing so, as some are valuable and should not be changed in any way.

If you ask a clock dealer how much your clock is worth, he will always under-value it – in case you turn around and ask him to buy it off you! He has to make a profit, the bigger the better, so if you are going to sell, please ask more than one dealer. If you are very lucky and have a valuable old piece, think about selling it at an auction. I have always found that when vintage clocks are sold at auctions, they fetch fair prices.

Heart, Hands and Face

The Movement

The quartz movements I have used in this book are quite easy to find in model shops, and are often advertised in hobby magazines.

This basic equipment is always measured in millimetres, and you should follow this. I have also given imperial measurements for wood, formica and other sundries. As the movement is not specified in imperial measurements by the suppliers, I have left it in metric here. If you want further information and an interesting catalogue, see the section on suppliers on page 48).

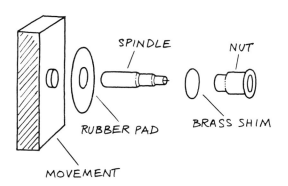

SPINDLE

NUT

RUBBER PAD

BRASS SHIM

MOVEMENT

These compact movements are driven by a small battery which lasts about 18 months, and they are amazingly accurate – they have an accuracy of 60 seconds a year. There are several different sizes available to suit the particular job in hand. The size of the movement relates to the power of your clock. The bigger the movement, the longer and heavier the hands can be. One of about 60mm × 60mm will drive hands up to 140mm long, which will give you a dial diameter of 300mm (12″). This is as large as most kitchen clocks. They can also be found as small as 46mm × 46mm, and only 13mm thick. These small ones will only drive hands up to 50mm long, but they are perfect for some of the miniature clocks in this book.

Quartz movements are very adaptable: they will run whichever way up you put them, and are not too sensitive to damp or heat. You could put one in a bathroom or near a cooker with no adverse effects.

The Spindle

The spindle is the shaft that sticks out of the middle of the movement, and to which the hands are fixed. It is also the most delicate and vulnerable part: it consists of a second shaft, which is located inside a minute tube, which in turn is inside an hour tube, yet the whole object is only 5mm (1/5″) in diameter. Around the bottom is a hollow nut which holds the movement to the dial.

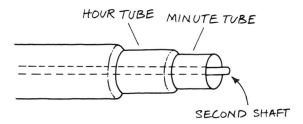

HOUR TUBE   MINUTE TUBE

SECOND SHAFT

As the spindle has to go through the dial and stick out enough on the other side for the hands to be fitted onto it, the length of the spindle is an important factor to bear in mind. If it is too long, the distance between the hands and the clock face will be too big, and will look very clumsy. If it is too short, it will not go through the dial and you will not be able to fit the hands. The thickness of the dial is the controlling factor. If you have a thick dial, you will need a long spindle movement, and for a thin dial, a short spindle movement. The thickness will also affect what material you use; in fact the thickest dial I have ever been able to use was 10mm (⅜″), and that left very little room for the hands.

Ordinary movements cost under £5 each, but if you want a pendulum it will cost about £9, and a chiming model will cost more still. Prices are greatly reduced if you buy more than one. Movements come with a protective rubber backing washer, a centre fixing nut, a brass shim and a hanging device to attach them to a wall. They do not, however, come with hands or a battery.

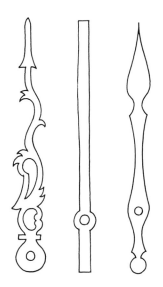

A SELECTION OF HANDS

The Hands

Hands can be obtained from the same supplier as the movements, are available in a variety of patterns, and should be chosen to suit your particular clock. Simple baton hands are best suited to modern clocks, but a range of ornate serpentine hands are also available if you are after a vintage look. Usually you will only use two hands, but you can fit a second hand if you like. If you don't use a second hand, you will need to fit a blank, which fits over the end of the spindle, looks like a drawing pin head, and looks neater than an open spindle.

Hands are very delicate and far too accurate for us to imitate. You should therefore always buy hands, and not try to make them yourself.

They can be altered, however, in various ways. You can shorten them, or stick extensions on them for extra width. Whatever you do, keep the weight to a minimum. A tiny shell or a paper pattern should be fine, but significant extra weight will shorten the life of the battery and the movement, and should be avoided.

Baton hands can be cut with pincers or scissors but other hands, notably serpentine hands, can look very strange indeed when shortened.

Hands can also be painted with enamel paint, which you can get in tiny little pots from most toy and model shops. Thread the hands onto a piece of wire and hang them up where they can dry, *before* you paint them. This will make life much easier and leave your hands and clothes much cleaner. Do not use too much paint; it is far better to use two thin coats, gently sanding the first one to give you a smoother finish.

The Dial

Dials are also available from the same supplier, and can give your clock a most professional look. I think, however, that it is more fun in many cases to make your own. If you do, then you can buy self-adhesive numerals from most good stationers, or clock suppliers.

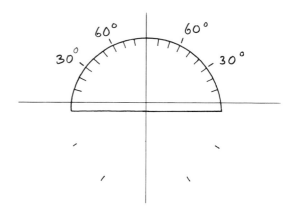

Many clocks do not need a dial at all, as we can read the time without them. Some will only need the four main points marked, and some all twelve. To mark the four main points is, of course, very easy. All you need to do is draw a cross to find the position of 12, 3, 6 and 9. If you need to find all twelve, draw a straight horizontal line. Then, with a protractor mark 30° and 60° on the left and right of the line, and above and below, as shown in the diagram. If you have done this accurately, you will have twelve points.

There is another good way of finding the twelve points, but you will need a compass. On a piece of paper, draw a circle the size of your dial. Without altering the spread or angle of your compass at all, put the sharp point anywhere on the circumference and draw another circle. The second circle will intersect the first one in two places. Again being careful not to alter the spread of your compass, move the sharp point to one of the intersections and draw another circle. Keep drawing circles round the first circle, using intersections as starting points for new circles, until you have returned to the second circle. Now draw a line from each intersection to the centre point, and you will have your twelve points.

To transfer these points to the dial, lay the paper over the dial, and do not let it move. Take a hammer and nail; hold the nail over one of the points and give it a sharp tap. Repeat this on all twelve points. Don't worry about the slight dents caused by this – they will be covered up by the numerals. Obviously this method will not work for glass or china. For china you should use carbon paper, and for glass you must place the paper dial *under* the glass and stick numerals over the points.

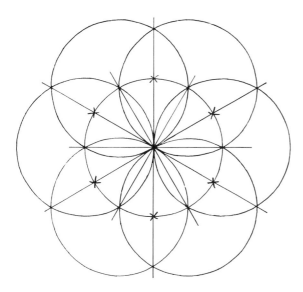

USING A COMPASS TO MARK
THE TWELVE POINTS

The Numerals

There are three sorts of numerals: Roman, Arabic, or just ticks. Roman numerals are always arranged as if you were standing in the middle to read them, so a VI is actually seen as IΛ. Also, by tradition, the 4 is written as IIII, not IV. All very confusing! Arabic numbers are much simpler as they are always read the right way up, and ticks are even simpler because they are not read at all. A word of warning; take great care in positioning the numerals correctly – it affects the finished appearance enormously, and it *does* affect how accurately you can tell the time. Numerals can be stuck on to most surfaces with a clear plastic glue, such as Bostic, and clock suppliers and stationery shops often stock self-adhesive numbers.

Fitting the Movement

Most of this information applies to all the clocks in this book, and rather than repeat myself I will refer you back to this page. The movement is held in place by a nut, 10mm external diameter, which passes through the dial and into the movement. As the fixing relies on the dial, the dial must be rigid. The fixing nut is actually hollow, so that the spindle can pass through it. The 10mm (⅜") hole, which you will be required to make in your dial, should be as neat and accurate as possible, as the flange of the nut is very small and it will not cover up any mistakes. If you *do* make a mistake, however, it is possible to place a thin washer between the nut and the front of the dial. This will cover up slight imperfections.

When the clock is ready for the movement to be fitted, put the rubber pad next to the movement and push the spindle through the dial. From the other side, you now push on the thin brass shim and then the nut. Screw the nut on tight. It is often easier at the end to hold the nut and screw the movement rather than vice versa. Normally it will not matter which way up the movement finishes, but obviously if it has to fit into a U box, then it will matter. U boxes are three-sided wooden frames, built on to the back of hanging clocks to protect the movement. Particularly if your clock has a pendulum, you should have a U box to ensure that it can swing unobstructed.

Fitting the Hands

There is a hole at one end of each hand which fits firmly over the spindle. This holds them in place. If you have painted the hands, please leave them to dry completely before fitting them.

When they are ready, prepare to fit the hour hand first. This is a press fit – you press it gently into position on the hour tube – and it should go as near to the dial as possible without touching the numbers. The minute hand may have a slot and a nut rather than a round hole. If it has, make sure that it is parallel to the hour hand before you secure it to the minute tube with the nut. If you decide to have a second hand, this goes on last, fitting over the fine pin right in the middle of the spindle. This pin is thin and will bend if you are not careful, so with great care press on the second hand with your finger. You may wish to decorate these hands further or stick small objects on them. These must be extremely light. Also, if the objects stick out, then only the minute hand can have them, as the hour hand has to pass under the minute hand once every hour, and of course you can't have a second hand.

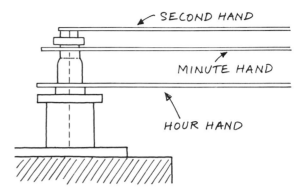

On the back of the movement there is a little wheel for setting the time. Press your finger on it and turn. This will turn the hands. Keep turning while you carefully check that the hands do not touch each other or anything else. If they do, just bend them a little so that they clear. When you are sure that they do not touch, put in the battery, set the right time, and there you are.

EASY
CLOCK PROJECTS

A Mantelpiece Clock

With a few simple materials, you can imitate a grand mantelpiece clock in the tradition of the great Victorian clockmakers who used marble and slate. Your supplies, however, could be begged from any builder on site. The best bet is where an older property is being renovated.

You will need:
450mm (18″) of 50mm (2″) height Ogee architrave
100mm (4″) of 100mm (4″) diameter plastic drain pipe
100mm × 210mm (4″ × 9″) of plywood 3mm (⅛″) thick
240mm (10″) of 150mm (6″) height Torus skirting board
dial of your choice, or separate numerals
short spindle movement
set of serpentine hands, hour hand 35mm, minute hand 46mm

Tools:
saw
glue
fine sand paper
10mm drill bit
2 No. 4 or 6 screws, 16mm (⅝″) or 20mm (¾″)
Polyfilla
black board paint
(a fret saw would make this easier)

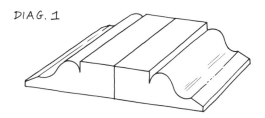

DIAG. 1

1 Saw the architrave into four pieces, each 100mm (4″) long. Glue two pieces together, as shown in diagram 1. Repeat this with the other two pieces.

2 The plastic pipe needs to be sanded to make the paint stick to it. You should do this with fine sand paper, always working round and round the pipe. Then, draw a straight line down the pipe, from one end to the other. On this line drill two holes. They should be 2–3mm (⅛″) in diameter, and 12mm (½″) from each end. You will need these holes later in order to screw the pipe to the skirting board.

3 Stand the pipe upright on the plywood. Using the inside of the pipe as a stencil, draw two circles on the wood, making sure that they do not overlap. Cut, outside the pencil lines, the two circles of wood, either with a fret saw or else with a series of straight cuts which you can then smooth off with sand paper. Eventually, the two wooden discs should fit tightly into the pipe.

4 Mark the centre of one of the discs. This will be the face and it needs to be very accurate. I always use the following method. Take a sheet of paper and fold it as shown in diagram 2A. Crease it and then open it out again. You will now have two angles of 45°. Lay the disc of wood on the paper over the crease, so that it fits into the corner but does not overlap the paper, as in diagram 2B. Now draw a line on the wood directly over the crease. Rotate the disc through 90° and repeat this process. If you have done this correctly, and please double check, then the intersection of the two lines will be the centre. Through the centre drill a 10mm (⅜″) hole.

5 Draw a line down the middle of the skirting board, and screw the pipe to it, using 16mm (⅝″) or 20mm (¾″) No. 4 or 6 screws through the holes which you have already drilled. See diagram 3. Put a little glue on the large flat undersides of the pieces of architrave, and push them into place alongside the pipe. They should be wedged in snugly under the pipe. The disc with the hole in it can now be glued into the pipe, but make sure that it is set in 2mm (⅛″) back from the edge of the pipe.

DIAG. 3

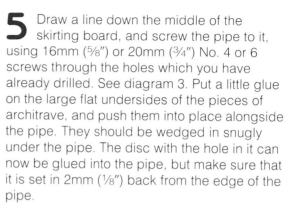

6 When all the glue has set, sand off any rough edges. Mix about two tablespoons of Polyfilla as directed on the packet, and smooth it into any cracks or gaps, and all the wood grain on the discs but *not* the central hole. When this is dry, sand it off with fine sand paper. Repeat this process until you have a perfectly smooth finish. Paint the clock all over with a blackboard paint. If necessary, sand it down again and repaint. When dry, buff it up with a soft duster and black shoe polish.

7 You could stick a ready-made dial with numbers to the face, but I think that simple Roman numerals look far grander. The movement and hands are fitted in the usual way, as described on p. 15.

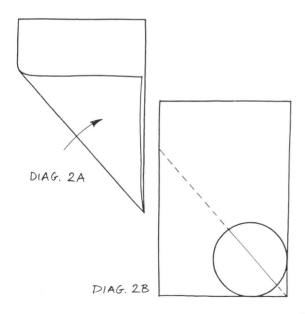

DIAG. 2A

DIAG. 2B

Wall Clock with Pendulum

It is not only lofty old grandfather clocks that can have brass pendulums swinging gracefully below their faces. Pendulums are available with quartz movements too, and the clock we are about to make is particularly suited to them. As ever, you must choose your own materials, and vary from my choice as much as you like. This is only a basic formula and you should experiment as much as you like. This clock could indeed imitate an old wooden clock, but it could just as easily make a bright and modern clock with a difference. Try sticking an interesting little *objet trouvé* to the base of the pendulum in keeping with the design of the face, perhaps a small shell or coin. Be careful not to overload it, though, or it will not swing.

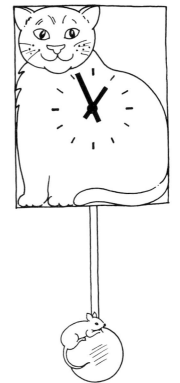

You will need:
450mm (18″) length of wood, 12mm ×
    32mm (½″ × 1¼″)
150mm × 230mm (6″ × 9″) piece of
    plywood or coloured formica, 3mm
    (⅛″) thick (this could be any shape you
    like, in fact. If you have a jig saw, now
    is the time to experiment with it. A
    hexagon can look spectacular.)
125mm (5″) dial
set of hands
quartz pendulum movement

Tools:
saw
'G' clamp, or about 1 metre (3′) of string
    and a 75mm (3″) nail
10mm drill bit
sand paper
glue
paint/varnish if you like

1 First of all make a U box from the length of wood. Cut the wood into two pieces 150mm (6″) long, and two pieces 62mm (2½″) long. Lay the four pieces in a rectangle on your work surface, as shown in diagram 1. Take one of the short pieces, put some glue on both ends, and put it back into the rectangle. Clamp it firmly and leave it to dry. If you don't have a clamp, use a 'Spanish Windless', which is very easy to make: wind a piece of string three or four times around the long sides of the rectangle, as shown in diagram 2. Put a 75mm (3") nail through the loop formed by the string, and twist it until the string is taut. Turn the nail around so that it touches the wood and cannot unwind.

DIAG. 1

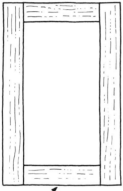

LEAVE BOTTOM PIECE UNGLUED

DIAG. 2

2 Now make the centre hole: on the plywood or formica, draw a pencil line down the centre. This is a vertical clock, so the sides are 230mm (9") and the top and bottom are 150mm (6"). Mark the point 75mm (3") down the centre line from the top. Drill a 10mm (⅜") hole through this point. If you are using plywood rather than formica, you should now sand it down and paint it with good undercoat. Repeat this until the surface is totally smooth.

3 Remove the wooden rectangle from the clamp or 'Spanish Windless'. The small piece of wood which was not glued should slip out to leave you with a perfect U box.

4 Pass the spindle through the hole in the board, and attach the movement as instructed on p. 15. Position the U box around the movement with the open side down and glue it in place to the board.

5 You can decorate your clock face in any way you like. You could use stencils, transfers, or even self-adhesive Roman numerals. On a clock of this size, it is perfectly easy to tell the time without numerals, and if your design would look better without them, then don't use them.

6 Finally, fit the hanging device provided, and the hands. As the pendulum is only for show, and doesn't have any effect on the speed of the clock, it can be any length you like. Hang the pendulum last of all, and always keep the clock upright after that. If you ever want to move the clock, take the pendulum off first.

Parrot Clock

Here is a parrot clock I originally made for a small child, but I have since been asked to make two for a very modern kitchen. Wherever it goes, it is an eyecatching, colourful design. Remember, though, that the pendulum is for effect only, and doesn't have anything to do with the speed of the movement. It is fun, all the same, to have this bright green tail swinging from side to side on a wall. You will need a jig saw and some off-cuts of formica, which you can get from any DIY shop. Choose whichever strong, simple colours you like, although I have suggested red, yellow, green, blue and black.

You will need:
350mm (18″) length of wood, 12mm × 32mm (½″ × 1¼″)
selection of formica off-cuts
pendulum quartz movement
set of baton hands
stick-on numerals (optional)

Tools:
sheet of A3 paper
scissors
jig saw
Clear Bostic, or similar glue
sand paper
compass
10mm drill

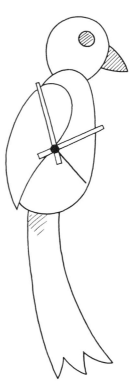

1 Cut the length of wood into two pieces 100mm (4″) long, and two pieces 65mm (2½″) long. Make a U box out of them, as directed for the *Wall Clock with Pendulum* on p. 20.

2 Draw your design full size on the sheet of A3 paper. You can use the basic pattern here, or change the shapes and colours as you please. Always make sure, however, that the pattern is big enough to cover the movement and its surrounding U box. Mark on your drawing the position of the movement, and the limits of the pendulum's swing.

3 Now cut out the paper design very accurately with a pair of scissors, and use it as a template to mark the formica with. When you have cut out all the formica as you are about to be instructed, you should end up with five pieces all of which overlap, so that they can be stuck together easily. It is vital that you follow these instructions to the letter. First, lay the paper pattern on the back of the black formica, and draw round the beak and head only, as shown in diagram 1. Remove the paper, and cut off the beak and tail from the paper itself, as in diagram 2. Leave the marked formica aside for the time being. Second, lay the paper pattern on the back of the yellow formica, and draw round the head and top part of the body. Remove the pattern and cut the head off it. Third, place the paper on the back of the blue formica and draw round the body. Again remove the paper, and this time cut the wing off it. Fourth, lay the paper wing on the back of the red formica, and draw round that. Finally, draw the tail on the back of the green formica. It is important that you draw the tail about 25mm (1") longer at the top than the pattern, so that it can extend behind the body and be attached to the pendulum movement.

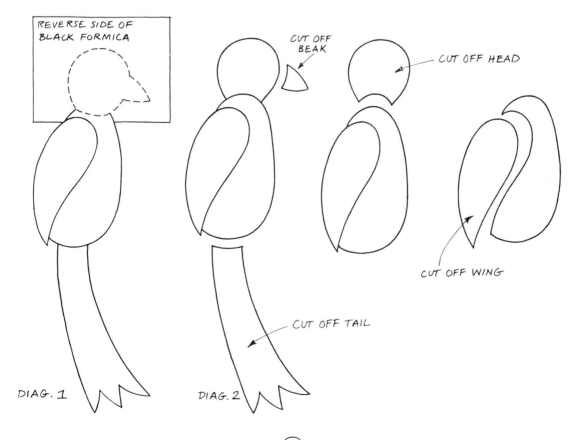

REVERSE SIDE OF BLACK FORMICA

CUT OFF BEAK

CUT OFF HEAD

CUT OFF WING

CUT OFF TAIL

DIAG. 1

DIAG. 2

4 All your formica is now marked, so clear your work surface and get ready to saw the shapes out. Make sure that you can hold the formica pieces firmly, right on the edge of your table. When using a jig saw, it is vital to wear protective goggles, and do not let the foot of the saw jump away from the work, as this can cause chipping and lead to nasty cuts. Cut the formica pieces just outside the pattern lines, so that you can sand back to them accurately afterwards.

5 When all the shapes are cut out, they should look like the pieces in diagram 3. Glue all, except the tail, together with clear glue. Leave this to dry under a heavy weight.

6 Stick the tail to the pendulum so that the top is about 15mm (½″) below the hook. You will also need to stick a coin, preferably a 2p piece, on the back of the bottom of the tail. This will weight it sufficiently.

7 After the glue is dry, sand the edges well. Decide where the centre hole is to be, and with a compass draw a circle about 75mm (3″) diameter centre on that point. Drill the centre hole to 10mm (⅜″). Mark the 12 points of your clock face on the circle, and stick on the numerals if you want them. Fit the movement and the hands as shown on p. 15, and carefully hang on the pendulum. When you hang it up, if the pendulum touches the wall, you can gently bend the tail forwards until it clears it safely.

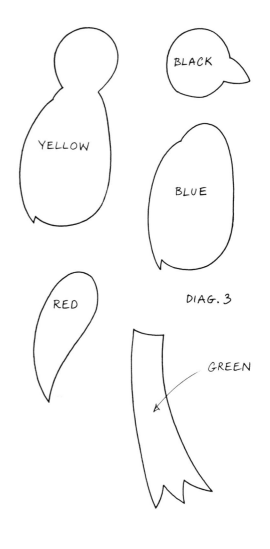

Opposite: Curtain Ring Clocks (pages 38–40)
Overleaf: Domino Clock (pages 30–31), Electrotime Sculpture Clock (page 41) and 'Dial-a-Dial' (page 46)
Facing page 25: Fabric Clock (pages 26–27)

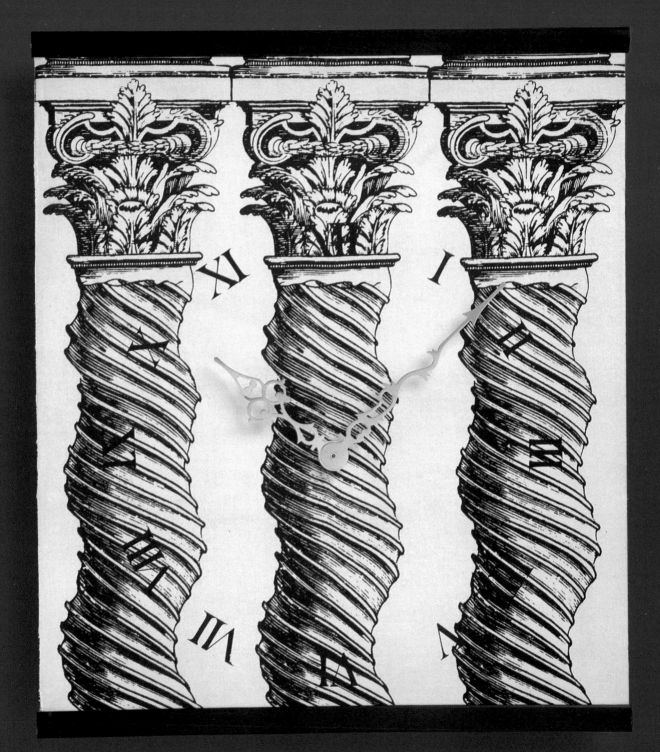

A Novel Kitchen Clock

These days so many foods come in attractive wooden boxes, and it seems a shame to throw them away. This is a wonderful way of putting them to good use. I have used a French cheese box, but you could use almost any fairly sturdy box. You might even have brought it back from a trip abroad, and perhaps it will remind you of a special meal or place . . .

FILL WITH POLYFILLA

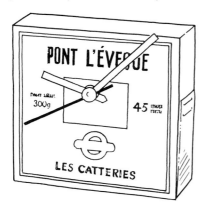

PONT L'ÉVÊQUE

PONT L'ÉVÊQUE
300g

45 mm

LES CATTERIES

You will need:
an interesting box (not too shallow, or it won't stand up!)
clear polyurethane varnish
piece of cardboard
Polyfilla
short spindle movement
set of baton hands, and a second hand

Tools:
small paint brush
round bladed knife
10mm drill bit

1 Give the box a good coat of polyurethane varnish, top, sides and bottom. When dry, place the bottom part on a table, and wedge a piece of cardboard into it, about 25mm (1″) from, and parallel to, what is to be the bottom of the clock. See diagram. Mix up a little Polyfilla as directed on the packet; for a small cheese box, you will only need about 4–6 tablespoons. Using a rounded knife blade, fill the space between the cardboard and the bottom of the clock. This will give the clock enough weight to stand up.

2 Drill a 10mm (⅜″) hole through the lid of the box in the middle, or if you think it would look better, why not incorporate it into the design of the label. Be careful not to drill too near to the edge of the lid, or the movement will not fit on the other side.

3 Paint the hands a strong colour that will show up against the label. I don't think that these clocks need numbers, but if you like you could mark 12, 3, 6 and 9 with coloured drawing pins or stickers.

4 Fit the movement to the lid, as described on p. 15. Fit the hands and the battery. Put the two parts of the box together again, and there you are!

Fabric Clock

This is, above all, a theme clock. You can make it as bold and outrageous or as soft and elegant as you like. It all depends upon what cloth you choose. I found some interesting black and white cloth with pillars printed on it, so I turned my clock into a mini classical temple. A delicate chintz with a pair of brass serpentine hands would also look lovely. The main point is to find some cloth with a definite centre. You might even decide to embroider your own cloth. If you don't like cloth, a picture painted on card is just as suitable.

You will need:
piece of clear rigid plastic, 150mm (6")
   square (not more than 3mm (⅛") thick)
piece of card, the size and shape of your
   intended clock
piece of cloth, about 300mm (12")
   square, with sides edged
2 poster hangers
long spindle movement
set of hands to match your cloth

Tools:
compass
pair of scissors
protractor or right angle
piece of paper, about 150mm (6") square
some string, at least 1 metre (3') long

1 Place the clear plastic on your work surface and mark the centre approximately with a compass point. Using the compass, draw a circle about 65mm (2½")

diameter on the plastic, and then cut this circle out. If you have not got a compass, a small bowl or saucer would do, but that will make it a little difficult to find the exact centre point later on. If you do need to use this method, however, you can find the centre using the method described on p. 19 for the *Mantelpiece Clock*.

2 Using the pointed end of your scissors, bore a hole through the exact centre of the plastic disc. It should be about 10mm (⅜") in diameter, so that it just fits over the spindle of the movement.

3 With a compass and protractor, draw a clock face on a piece of paper. All you need to show is a circle with numerals in it. The circle should be the same diameter as the plastic disc. This piece of paper is only going to be used as a pattern to trace from, so it doesn't need to look at all attractive, but it does need to show the position of the numerals as accurately as possible. Remember that there are 30° between each of the twelve numerals, and 90° between each of the four main ones.

4 Lay the plastic over the paper clock face, and use the latter as a guide for where to position the numerals on the plastic. You can use ready-made, self-adhesive numerals or you can draw them on, but you must position them mirrorwise, because you are sticking them on to the back of the face and it will eventually have to be turned over. This is a little tricky at first, and it's a good idea to practise on an offcut. Refer to diagram 1.

DIAG. 1

5 Take the card, mark the centre of the dial, and cut a 10mm (⅜″) hole through it, so that the spindle can pass through it.

6 Cut the string so that it is 3 times as long as one of the poster hangers. Knot the two ends together and thread the string through the hanger. Make sure that the knot is inside the hanger so that it cannot be seen.

7 Lay the card on the table and place the cloth on it, with the centre of the dial directly over the hole in the middle of the card. Keeping the cloth as flat and steady as you can, slide the two hangers over the card and cloth. The hanger with string in it should be at the top. See diagram 2.

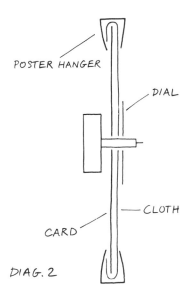

POSTER HANGER

DIAL

CLOTH

CARD

DIAG. 2

8 Push the spindle through the hole in the card, and ease it through the weave of the cloth. If you have used a painting instead of cloth, you will have to pierce a small hole in it. Now, lay the plastic on the cloth, numbered side down, and with the spindle through the hole. Secure this 'sandwich' with the centre nut, as described on p. 16. Attach the hands, insert the battery, and hang up your clock.

A Plate Clock

Finding an interesting plate is not too difficult – in fact you probably already have one lurking at the bottom of an old box in a garage or an attic. If not, don't despair, because half the fun of this clock is having an excuse to visit junk shops and market stalls, if you need an excuse. Don't forget, while you are there, to keep your eyes open for other odds and ends that would make an unusual clock. Alternatively, you could personalise the clock with initials, perhaps even a wedding date. Having found your plate, you may feel that drilling a hole in it is a bit beyond you. Never mind, any glass merchant can do it for you, and that will prove far cheaper than buying the necessary drills. If, however, you are prepared to have a go at drilling, then please follow the instructions very carefully. I strongly suggest that you practise a couple of times on a plate that doesn't matter.

You will need:
plate
long reach movement
set of hands to suit your plate

Tools:
masking tape
1–1½kg (2–3lbs) of wet sand
handful of putty
electric drill (*Non Hammer*)
3mm or 4mm masonry drill bit
cupful of three-in-one oil
10mm masonry drill bit

1 Stick a piece of masking tape over the approximate centre of the plate, and then mark the exact centre with a pencil. You can find the centre using the method described for the *Mantelpiece Clock* on p. 19. For plates, however, I always use the following method. Take a long thin piece of wood – it must be at least 100mm (4″) longer than the diameter of the plate. Drive two nails halfway into the wood as shown in diagram 1. The heads should

DIAG. 1

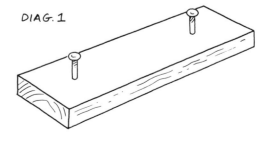

protrude by about an inch and the distance between them should be a little less than the diameter of the plate. Slide the plate between the nails until it is firmly in contact with both of them. Holding it carefully in this position, draw a line on the masking tape, using the wood as a ruler. See diagram 2. Rotate the plate through 90° and draw another line. Repeat this process twice more as shown in diagram 3 and you should be left with a little square on

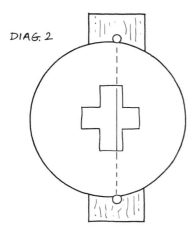

DIAG. 2

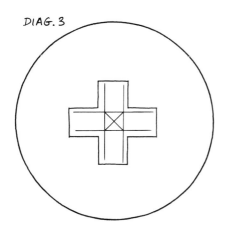

DIAG. 3

the masking tape. Draw two diagonal lines through this, and the intersection will be the centre.

2 Put the wet sand in a pile at least 100mm (4″) high on your work surface. Settle the plate into it, face side up, so that it is completely supported by the sand. Work the putty in your fingers until it is smooth, and then mould it into a little circular wall, about 7mm (¼″) high, around the central area where you are going to drill. Using a 3mm or 4mm masonry bit, *not on Hammer Action or your plate will shatter*, start your hole. The masking tape should stop the drill from skidding sideways, but be prepared to hold it firmly. As soon as the drill bites into the plate, stop. Now fill your little wall with oil, and continue drilling. You can press quite hard until the last moment, when you must ease up to make the final break-through. Turn the plate over, resettle it in the sand, reform your putty wall and fill it with more oil. Using the 10mm drill bit, start drilling from the back. As soon as the full width of the drill is cutting, stop. Turn the plate over again, rebuild your putty wall and fill it with oil. Now you can drill right the way through.

3 Clean off your plate and mount the movement, as instructed on p. 15. When you put the hands on, they may have to be bent forward at the tip, so that they can clear the rim of the plate. Try to do this either as a gentle curve or a positive corner, but not as a mixture of both, which looks terrible.

4 Your movement will come with an attachment to hang it from a wall. This can now be attached, and the battery fitted.

Domino Clock

Using dominoes as numerals is an inspired idea: each piece marks an hour on the face, and the numbers on it also add up to that hour. It is also a versatile idea – a chance for a flash of bright colour for a workshop or a nursery, or a chic, restrained design in black and white for a more formal environment. The overall appearance is distinctive and professional, and yet the whole project can be assembled in about an hour.

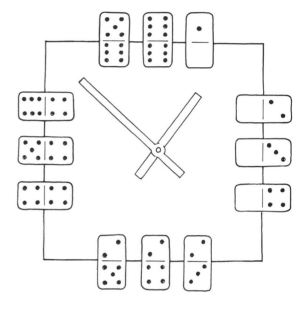

You will need:
150mm–230mm (6"–9") square of colour:
    tile (ceramic or cork)/off-cut of
    formica/painted plywood
set of dominoes
movement
set of baton hands

Tools:
10mm drill bit
Clear Bostic

1 If you have decided to use a ceramic tile, this will give you the best and certainly the most 'finished' effect, but it involves some fairly complicated drilling. If you *do* choose to drill through a tile, use the method described for *Plate Clock* on p. 28. Alternatively, most glass cutters would be happy to drill through a tile for you. For all other materials, decide how big you want your clock face to be, and cut your colour square to size. Smaller than

150mm (6") square will make the dominoes look cramped, and larger than 230mm (9") square will make them appear insignificant. Mark the middle of your square by drawing two diagonal lines from corner to corner as shown in diagram 1: the centre is where the two lines meet. Drill a 10mm (⅜") hole through this point.

2 Select which dominoes you want to choose. This is a little more complicated than it seems, because there are several ways of showing each number. Eight, for example, could be 2 & 6, 3 & 5, 4 & 4, 5 & 3 or 6 & 2. Then decide where you want to position them. I have gone for a discreet, elegant look by making the

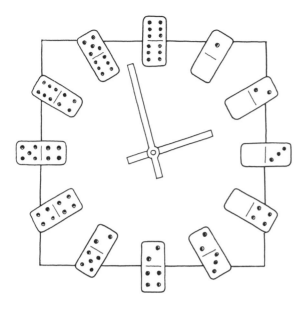

central line on the dominoes coincide with the edge of the clock, as in the first drawing, but you could spread them out more, or even have them at an angle to the square. Play around with them until you are sure about what you would like best. If you decide to have them mainly on the surface of the square, and not overlapping the edge, then please remember to use a long spindle movement so that the hands do not hit the dominoes.

3 Mark with a pencil where you want the dominoes to be positioned, and then glue them in place with Clear Bostic or any clear plastic glue. Before the glue sets, make sure that the dominoes are all in the right position.

4 Paint the hands a colour which matches the clock. When the paint and the glue are dry, mount the movement and hands, and attach the hanging device, as instructed on p. 15.

Perspex Sun Clock

Perspex is one of the most versatile materials for making clocks. It comes in a multitude of different colours, and can be cut into a variety of shapes. If you have a fret saw you can achieve intricate designs, but a hack saw and sandpaper is all you will need for this clock. Here a yellow sun forms the centre of the clock and cloud shapes are stuck on above. The blue background is heated and bent back at the bottom to form a stand.

You will need:
300mm × 230mm (12″ × 9″) piece of blue perspex
150mm × 230mm (6″ × 9″) piece of white perspex
100mm × 100mm (4″ × 4″) piece of yellow perspex
long spindle movement
set of plain baton hands

Tools:
pair of dividers
fret or hack saw
sandpaper (very fine wet and dry)
odd piece of thick wood, at least 370mm
    × 370mm (15″ × 15″)
8 nails
hammer
electric drill (10mm drill bit)
75mm (3″) tank cutter (drill attachment)
gas cooker or burner
Araldite

1 First of all, make the basic shape of the clock. Take the blue perspex and mark the centre point of one of the short sides. Mark a point 115mm (4½″) in. Using that point as the centre, scratch a semi-circle with a pair of dividers. This semi-circle will touch both the long sides and one of the short sides as shown

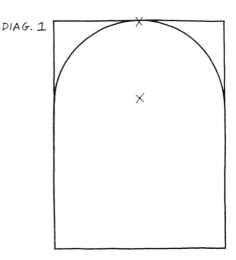

DIAG. 1

in diagram 1. Lay the perspex flat on a workbench and cut along the semi-circle using a fret saw or a hack saw. If you are using a hack saw, make a series of straight cuts and smooth it off with sandpaper. Finish the curve by polishing it with very fine wet and dry.

2 Cut the white perspex into the shape of clouds. You can follow the patterns given here (diagram 2), or vary them as you like. Again, use a fret saw, or a hack saw and sand paper.

DIAG. 2

3 To make the central sun shape, you will need a thick piece of wood to act as a base on which to cut the yellow perspex. Put it on the floor and stand a heavy table or other piece of furniture on it to keep it steady. Lay the yellow perspex on the centre of the wood and hold it firmly in place by driving two nails on each of the four sides so that their heads secure the perspex. Take your drill and the 75mm (3") tank cutter, and very gently cut out the yellow disc.

4 Now the exciting part – bending the blue perspex shape to make the base. Clear a space on a table or flat surface near your gas

cooker or burner. Have ready a piece of wood, or even a book: when the perspex is hot, you will use this to bend it back. Hold the perspex by the curved end and pass the other end back and forth across the flame, about 25mm (1") above it. Keep the perspex moving and turn it over as soon as it starts to curve. When it is soft, very quickly lay the piece on the table with the hot end overhanging by about 75mm (3"). Using the piece of wood or book, bend it down more than 90°, but no more than about 130°, and hold it there until it cools. This will leave you with a 230mm ×230mm (9" × 9") shape, slightly tilted back, as in diagram 3.

DIAG. 3

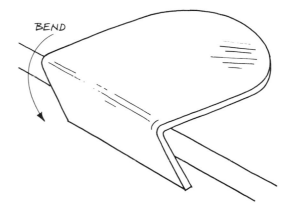

BEND

5 With Araldite, stick on the clouds and sun as shown in the illustration. Allow this to dry completely.

6 Lay the clock on the workbench and with a 10mm bit, drill through the centre of the sun. Insert the movement, as directed on p. 15, push in the battery, and you have a perspex sun clock.

Floral Clock

Have you ever been to a seaside resort or public garden where master gardeners have created a floral clock, with bulbs planted and seeds sown so that the twelve hours are represented by flowers of different colours? Well here is a chance to make your own 'growing' timepiece, a kitchen clock for a sunny window sill. Water it carefully so that the hands (and the battery below) do not get wet. It is not a good idea to use this method to make an outdoor flowerbed version, but a sheltered outdoor spot would be good.

For this clock you will need a selection of low-growing plants – some herbs would be suitable. A tall, wide yoghurt tub, about 90mm–120mm (3½"–4½") in diameter, makes a good base for your clock and can be painted to look like a pond.

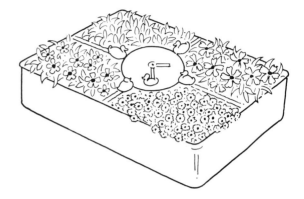

You will need:
yoghurt tub
blue paint
short spindle movement
small plastic ducks or similar to act as
    markers
set of baton hands (no longer than the
    radius of the yoghurt tub)
green seed tray or similar container
enough earth to fill the tray
selection of low-growing plants or seeds,
    such as dwarf petunias, French
    marigolds, alyssum

Tools:
scissors
glue
Stanley knife

1 First make a pond for the middle of your garden. This pond will actually house the movement. Remove the lid of the yoghurt pot and paint it blue. Through the middle drill a 10mm (⅜") hole, or bore one with a pair of scissors. Paint any part of the tub which will show above ground level.

2 Fit the movement to the lid with the centre nut, put in the battery, and put the lid back on the tub, making sure that it fits tight all round.

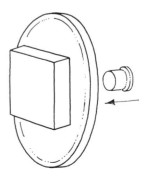

3 Around the edge of the lid you will need something to mark at least 12, 3, 6 and 9. Small yellow plastic ducks could be positioned on the edge of the lid.

4 Cut the hands to the right length and fix the hour hand. On the minute hand you could stick another small yellow duck or a fish.

clock is actually working. It can therefore be a little tricky fitting the hands, but be gentle and make sure straight away that the hands can turn without obstruction.

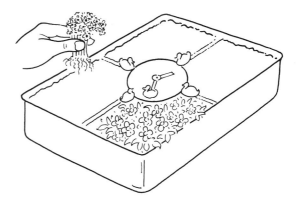

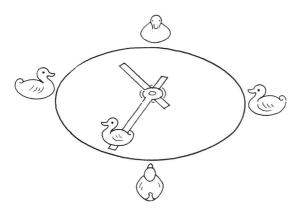

5 Attach the minute hand and centre plug, as directed on p. 16. Remember that the battery has already been fitted, and so the

6 Place the tub complete with clock in the middle of the tray, and fill the tray with sifted earth, pressing gently and firmly round the tub. Divide the garden into four segments and plant a different herb or annual in each.

Paper Clock

I was rummaging in a junk shop when I came across some crocheted doilies, and they struck me as just the thing for a clock. Then I noticed a rush table-mat, so I gathered up my loot and . . . ! Although I originally made this with crocheted doilies, I have since used paper ones, because they are more versatile. They can be cut or painted, or even handmade in the first place. Try having the background card a contrasting colour – a white doily on a pale blue card would look very pretty in a bedroom.

1 If you are going to make a doily, this is how. Take a clean sheet of A4 drawing paper. Fold it in half, and then in half again. Draw a line 30° out from each of the two folded edges, as shown in diagram 1. Fold one edge over on to the further line. Then turn the whole thing over and fold the other edge back. You should have a wedge of 30°. With strong scissors cut out a pattern; when it is unfolded, you will have a 12 faceted design, ready to be painted.

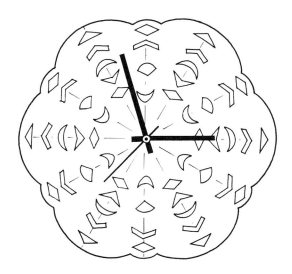

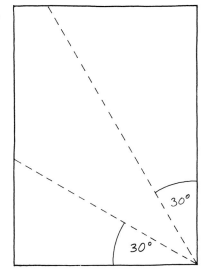

DIAG. 1

30°

30°

You will need:
two pieces of card
paper doily or sheet of A4 drawing paper
   to make doily
long spindle movement
set of suitable hands

Tools:
scissors
paper glue

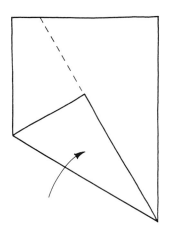

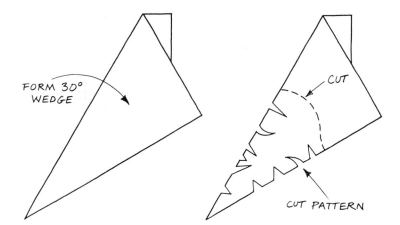

FORM 30°
WEDGE

CUT

CUT PATTERN

2 Cut out a piece of stiff card the size and shape of your doily, and paint it to contrast with the colour of the doily. In the centre, bore a 10mm (⅜″) hole with scissors for the spindle and nut. Spread a thin coat of glue on the card and lay the doily flat on it. Leave it all to dry.

3 When dry, mount the movement through the hole in the middle as shown on p. 15. You can either hang this on a wall, or make a stand out of the second piece of card, as shown in the diagram.

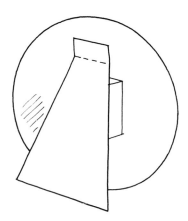

Curtain Ring Clock

This little clock is ideal for travelling, as it is light and strong, and the hands are well protected. When finished, it looks so professional that few people will realise it is made out of some simple curtain rings.

You will need:
75mm (3″) square of leather
Mini Hechinger movement; they are
   circular with a 48mm diameter
75mm (3″) square of hard wood, as thin
   as possible
4 wooden curtain rings 75mm (3″)
   diameter
3 No. 4 screws 15mm (5⁄8″)
50mm (2″) square of baize
set of gold antique hands, with the minute
   hand 25mm long

Tools:
piece of card, not smaller than 150mm
   (6″) square
small hammer
2mm drill bit
counter sink drill bit
clear glue
hack saw
screwdriver
Stanley knife
polyurethane varnish
paper clip
gold paint

1 Lay the leather on a piece of card, and over the centre of the leather hold the centre nut of the movement. Hit the nut gently

with a hammer so that it dents the leather. Now put the nut on a hard surface, turn the leather over, and lay it on top of the nut. The dent that you have just made should sit over the hole in the nut, as in diagram 1. With a light hammer, tap all round the nut and you will find that you have cut out the right sized hole in the leather. Do be gentle, or you will damage the screw thread.

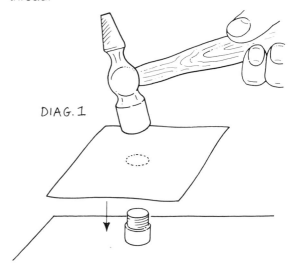

DIAG. 1

2 On the piece of hard wood, draw the centre line and mark the centre point. Drill a 2mm hole through the centre. Lay the wood flat and hold one of the rings upright on it, at right angles to the centre line. Position this ring on the centre line so that one side of the ring covers half of the hole in the wood, as shown in diagram 2. Without moving the ring from this position, mark the other side of the ring, as shown in the diagram. Repeat this process on the other side of the hole. Now drill through these two marks. Counter sink all three holes.

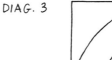

DIAG. 3

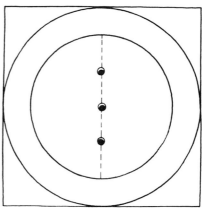

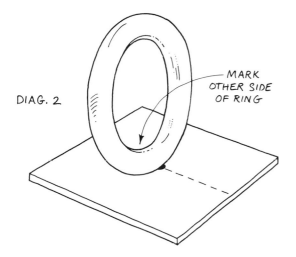

DIAG. 2

MARK
OTHER SIDE
OF RING

3 Lay the wood flat with the counter sinks up. Remove the little screw eye from one of the curtain rings and stick it onto the wood with a little clear glue, as in diagram 3. Make sure that the hole in the centre of the wood is also in the centre of the ring. If the wood is exactly 75mm (3″) sq. and the ring is exactly 75mm (3″) in diameter then, so long as you position the two accurately, the hole will automatically be in the middle of both. When the glue has dried, trim the wood to the curve of the ring.

4 Remove the screw eyes from the other three rings. Drive a 15mm (⅝″) No. 4 screw up through the centre hole in the wood and into the little hole left by the screw eye, as shown in diagram 4. Spread a thin line of clear glue on one side of another ring, press it on to the centre ring. Make sure that you position it over the centre line, so that the screw eye hole is directly above one of the holes in the wood. Again drive a screw up through the wood and into this ring. On the other side of the centre

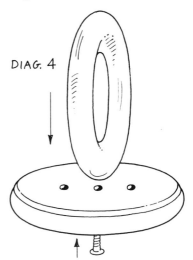

DIAG. 4

ring, spread a thin line of glue and lay the leather over it, shiny side out, being careful not to get any glue on the shiny side. The leather should be as taut as possible. Take the last ring and spread a thin line of glue on it, and stick it to the leather, and again position it so that you can drive a screw through the wood and into the screw eye. The leather should now be sandwiched between two rings.

5 When the glue has dried, trim away with a Stanley knife the leather that sticks out from between the two rings. Be careful not to scratch the rings. Paint all the wood with gloss polyurethane varnish. When this has dried, stick the baize on to the base, exactly as you stuck the leather onto a ring. Again wait for the glue to dry, and then trim off the excess baize.

6 Stir the gold paint thoroughly. Dip the tip of a straightened paper clip into the paint and touch the leather with it to make 12 small dots. It might be better to try this out first on an offcut of leather. When your numerals are painted and dried, fit the hands and the movement as instructed on p. 15. Make certain that the hands do not touch the inside of the rings. If they do, you can cut them with a sharp pair of scissors.

Variation

As a slightly less portable variation on this idea, you can make a different base. Take a 125mm (5") length of door architrave and drill two holes in it, 18mm (¾") diameter. The distance between these holes should be exactly the same as the width of the rings. Into the holes drive two 150mm (6") lengths of 18mm (¾") dowel. The clock can now be wedged and screwed in between the two posts. Take two acorns, as used on blind pulls, and stick them on to the posts as a final touch. Again, paint all the wood with gloss polyurethane varnish.

Electrotime Sculpture Clock

Here is a bit of fun for a room with a way-out look. If you can find a friendly electrician, you might be able to beg enough parts. They use conduit in three colours: black, white and an extremely lurid shade of orange. Plumbers use similar pipes for overflows, and their corners are neater. You can get T-pieces, elbows, straight joiners, and a whole range of other bits and pieces from which to construct a Hi-tec monstrosity.

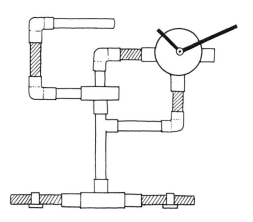

You will need:
selection of plastic electrical conduit, including at least one junction box
Junghans mini movement (a small circular one)
set of baton hands

Tools:
chisel or Stanley knife
10mm drill bit
fine-toothed saw

1 Inside the junction box there are some little bits which prevent the movement from going in as shown in diagram 1, so they must be cut out. You should be able to do this with a chisel or Stanley knife. If the plastic is too hard to be cut in this way, you can use an old knife blade which has been heated in a flame. Take care not to burn yourself.

2 Drill a 10mm (⅜") hole in the junction box and mount the movement, as directed on p. 15. Now you can spend hours entertaining yourself by building fantastic shapes with all the pieces of electrical conduit. If you need to shorten them, do so with a fine-toothed saw. Remember that this structure must stand up, so try not to overload any one side. If you do, you can correct the balance by filling the bottom pipes with sand. There are some useful clips (see diagram 2) that are used to hold the conduit to walls, which I have used as feet.

3 When you are satisfied with your toy, and when it is quite stable, fit the hands, as instructed on pp. 15–16.

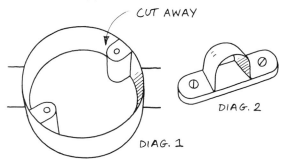

CUT AWAY

DIAG. 2

DIAG. 1

Hi-tec Clock

Structures made of very thin strips of wood can be great fun to make. They require no fancy equipment at all, and look extremely elegant, if a little bizarre and futuristic. They are also much stronger than you would expect. It is possible to buy 3mm (⅛″) and 6mm (¼″) square strips of hard wood, usually Ramin, from most model and DIY shops. This shape is a bit like a triangular easel, and it is certainly my favourite shape. Once you have got the idea, however, you can adapt it to any shape you like. Wooden strips are not expensive and you will find that you always need more than you think, so buy plenty. The structure that I have made here is based on three triangles. The advantage of this is that it always stands flat, but if you have four or more legs, you may have to fiddle about at the end to make them all equal length.

You will need:
3 metres (3 yards) of 3mm (⅛″) sq. hard
    wood (buy 4 metres/4 yards to be on
    the safe side)
short reach mini movement
large set of baton hands
drawing pin
silver paint

Tools:
pencil
ruler
sheet of A3 paper
board or table that you can push nails
    into without incurring the wrath of its
    owner
sticky tape
sharp Stanley knife
hack saw
packet of thin nails
white wood glue
sandpaper
(a fine-toothed tenon or gents saw is a
    help, but not necessary)

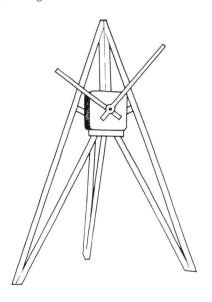

1 With a pencil and ruler, draw a triangle full size on a piece of A3 paper. Follow the pattern given here (diagram 1), and make sure you have the correct angles between the joints. It doesn't matter what length the sides are, but the angles are vital. With 4 metres (4 yards) of wood, the longest side should be about 350mm (14″) long. Once you have mastered this pattern, you can experiment.

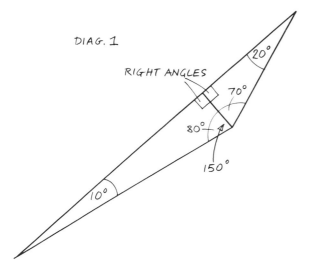

DIAG. 1

RIGHT ANGLES

20°
70°
80°
150°
10°

piece in place, again with nails on either side to hold it steady. Repeat this with each piece to complete the triangle. Make sure the nails are holding each joint tight. Leave it all to dry.

5 When the glue has set, remove the nails and lift off the triangle, without tearing the drawing. Now make another triangle . . . and another. When they are all dry, sand them smooth and glue two of them together, as shown in diagram 2.

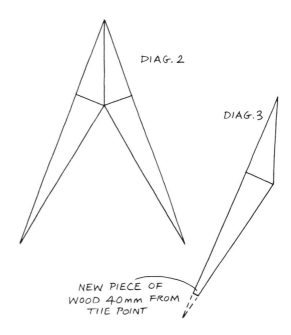

DIAG. 2

DIAG. 3

NEW PIECE OF WOOD 40mm FROM TI1E POINT

2 Lay the drawing on your board or table and fix it down with sticky tape. Take a length of wood and lay it on your drawing. With a Stanley knife mark the angle and position of each end of the drawing on the wood itself. Remove the wood and cut it at these marks with a hack saw, or fine-toothed tenon or gents saw. Repeat this process with each separate part of the triangle.

3 Lay the pieces of wood on the drawing again to make sure that you have cut them at exactly the correct angle and length. Using these pieces of wood as a pattern, cut two more of each, so that you have enough wood ready to make three triangles in all.

4 Take the longest piece, lay it on the drawing, and drive in two nails on either side to hold it firm. Slide a scrap of paper under each end; this will stop the wood from sticking to the drawing. Put a little glue on the angled end of your wood and stick the next

6 Stick a little piece of wood into the third triangle. This should be positioned horizontally, about 40mm (1½″) up from the bottom. When this has dried, cut the point of the triangle back to this piece of wood, as in diagram 3, and then glue this triangle to the back of the other two.

7 Make a crossbar for the movement to sit on. To do this, you stick a 50mm (2″) length of wood horizontally across the front triangle as in diagram 4. Put the hanging device into the movement upside down, so that it cannot be seen above the movement. Holding the movement in place on the crossbar, note where the hanger comes to, and push in a drawing pin at that point. Eventually, when the movement rests on the crossbar, the hanger will be hooked under this drawing pin for extra security. See the cross-sectional diagram 5.

8 Sand off the joints and paint all the wood with silver paint. I have used Hammerite; it is easily available and I like the finish it gives. The movement can now be fixed to the frame: hook it up under the drawing pin and slide it down onto the crossbar. I have left the hands black, but any primary colour against silver would look spectacular.

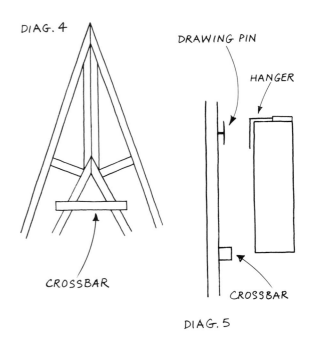

DIAG. 4

DRAWING PIN

HANGER

CROSSBAR

CROSSBAR

DIAG. 5

Once You Know How

Here are a few ideas to get you thinking and devising all sorts of ingenious clocks. Nature, Art, Science and junkshops everywhere are packed full of bric-a-brac crying out to be clockified. There are two points to bear in mind when choosing your materials. Firstly, the dial must be rigid or it will not support the movement. Secondly, the dial must be thin and relatively flat, so that the spindle can stick through far enough for the hands to be fitted. Spindles are not normally longer than 20mm, and this will limit your choice of material.

Portaclock

You can buy rubber suction pads at most hardware shops, and stick them onto the back of a lightweight movement. You could even stick one onto the back of the *Curtain Ring Clock* on p. 38. Do not fix it to the base. This can then be stuck onto a dashboard, a windscreen, a bathroom mirror, or anywhere you please.

Time and Tide

There are some large sea shells, scallop or oyster shells, cockles, that could be used as timepieces, because they are thin and flat. Drill a hole using the method for a plate on p. 29. This clock looks beautiful when mounted upright on a plate display stand.

Sign of the Times

Sometimes one 'acquires' a signpost, notice, plaque, or even a car licence plate that would be fun to keep. By adding a clock movement you can turn it into a real novelty. It is one of my life's ambitions to find a licence plate with TIM on it. This sort of clock would make a fun present for a teenager's room.

Playing for Time

One playing card is a bit too narrow, so cut a piece of card the size of two or three playing cards and then stick them onto it. Drill the centre hole to 10mm (3/8") and fit the movement. I have a clock with the centre hole through the middle of an Ace with two Kings on either side.

Lighting up Time

In the 60s there was a fashion for large, flat dish-shaped light fittings with designs radiating out from the centre. These dishes quite often turn up in market stalls, and are perfect for clocks. If the central hole is too big, reduce it with a washer. The dish-shape enables you to put the movement on the concave side, and it will hang flat against a wall.

Antiquarian

If you find or have a book that has an interesting cover but is totally useless inside, you can cut away the middle of the pages with a sharp Stanley knife, and mount a movement on the cover. A leatherbound book with brass serpentine hands looks most elegant.

Dial-a-Dial

Here is the ultimate, old-fashioned executive desktop gadget! Find an old dial phone, open it up, take out the wiring and remove the dial. Stick a clock dial on the front, with the movement and the battery already attached to it. Put on some hands and there you are.

Record Time

Old '78' records often have sentimental values which long outlast their quality as records. Sometimes they also have interesting labels. To preserve and display these feelings, enlarge the hole to 10mm (3/8") so that it can take the spindle. You could mark the hours with transfers of pop stars!

Big Ben

Some modern cupboard doors are so thin that it is possible to drill a 10mm (3/8") hole through a panel and fit a movement on the inside. Then the whole panel can be decorated to make a face, or even better, stick a photograph of Big Ben on the panel and mount the movement in the right place.

Tempo

For a music-lover, take a double cassette box and mount the movement inside so that it can be seen through the clear plastic on the other side. If you can find a cassette label with an appropriate name, such as 'The Dance of the Hours', so much the better.

Tools

Tools make life easier, and the more you have and the better they are, the easier life becomes. But this book does not require any specialist or complicated equipment. It is reasonable to assume that you will have access to an electric drill, and a hammer and some pliers. I have tried to keep within these limits, but occasionally you will need something else. Most of these you will find in a kitchen drawer, but others will have to be bought or borrowed. Most of them shouldn't, however, cost you more than a couple of pounds, such as a Stanley knife, which is essential for some clocks, and a 10mm drill bit which I have specified for almost every clock.

For the *Parrot Clock*, you will need a jig saw, which is not expensive. This is the only clock of this kind that I have included, but if you are the proud possessor of a jig saw and want to put it to greater use, there is no limit to the number of 'picture clocks' that you can make. Use the simple instructions given for the *Basic Wall Clock with Pendulum* or even the principle behind the *Parrot Clock* to make clocks out of wood, perspex, and formica shapes.

Another useful tool, which isn't actually essential, except for the *Perspex Sun Clock*, is a tank cutter. This is a drill attachment, and will enable you to cut holes or discs of various diameters in thin wood or plastic.

Perhaps more important than most of these tools is somewhere to work, where you have some peace and where you can leave half-finished work so that prying hands will not tamper with your delicate handiwork. This is a tall order in most homes, and you will have to improvise. A wooden board laid on a kitchen table, with some newspaper and a thick old dustsheet or blanket to protect the table, will make a perfectly adequate bench, and a large box to put things in is a must.

Suppliers

If you live in or around London, then a visit to Clerkenwell is a must, as this is the centre of the old clockmaking industry. Where St John Street crosses Clerkenwell Road you will find several shops that supply every conceivable clock part that you could imagine.

In larger towns, some model shops will stock what you need, but rather than run around the country looking for serpentine hands and long spindle movements, you should first of all consult a catalogue. H.S. Walsh have a comprehensive catalogue of clock materials, which includes every basic item that you will need. The catalogue costs £1 and you should send your cheque or postal order to the following address: H.S. Walsh, 243 Beckenham Road, Beckenham, Kent BR3 4TS.

This catalogue is also full of interesting information about clocks, and it may even encourage you to go on to the next stage, making your own movements.

Tools can, of course, be bought all over the place. Unless you are very short of money, do not be tempted by the very cheapest tools, as they are almost invariably the worst. The big DIY shops are often the best places for power tools, though sometimes the people at your local DIY/hardware shop are more prepared to stop and talk and advise you. In fact a friendly shop of this sort is an enormous help, particularly when you are having trouble with tools or supplies.